In God's Name

by
Sandy Eisenberg Sasso

and illustrated by
Phoebe Stone

Library of Congress Cataloging-in-Publication Data
Sasso, Sandy Eisenberg.
In God's Name / by Sandy Eisenberg Sasso;
illustrated by Phoebe Stone.
p.   cm.
ISBN 1-879045-26-5 : $16.95
1. Religion — Juvenile literature.
2. God — Name — Juvenile literature.
[1. God.]
I. Stone, Phoebe, date, ill.   II. Title.
BL92.S27 1994   94-18262
291.2'11—dc20   CIP
AC

10 9   8   7   6   5   4

Manufactured in the United States of America

For my mother and in memory of my father
who always listened
and
For Dennis
my partner in love and in faith
— S.S.

For David and Ethan with love
— P.S.

Published by
JEWISH LIGHTS Publishing
A Division of LongHill Partners, Inc.
PO Box 237
Sunset Farm Offices Route 4
Woodstock, Vermont 05091
Tel: (802) 457-4000   Fax: (802) 457-4004

The voice of God is in the uniqueness

of each and every person.

The Holy One said:

"Do not be confused because you hear many voices.

Know that I am One and the same."

Pesikta de Rav Kahana 12:25

After God created the world
all living things on earth
were given a name.
The plants and the trees,
the animals and the fish,
and each person,
young and old,
had a special name.

But no one knew
the name for God.

So each person searched
for God's name.

The farmer
whose skin was dark
like the rich brown earth
from which all things grew
called God
Source of Life.

The girl whose skin was as golden as the sun

that turned night into day

called God

Creator of Light.

The man who tended sheep in the valley

called God

Shepherd.

The tired soldier who fought too many wars

called God

Maker of Peace.

The artist who carved figures from the earth's hard stone

called God

My Rock.

Sometimes the people
who called God
by different names
were puzzled.

They said,
"Every living thing
has a single name:
the marigold,
pansy and lily;
the oak tree,
sequoia and pine.
God must have a
single name that is greater
and more wonderful
than all other names."

Each person thought his
name for God
was the greatest.
Each person thought her
name for God
was the very best.
The farmer who called God
Source of Life said,
"This is the true name
for God."
The girl who called God
Creator of Light insisted,
"This is the most splendid
name for God."
The shepherd, soldier
and artist believed
they each had the perfect
name for God.

But no one listened.
Least of all, God.

And so each person kept
searching for God's name.

The woman who cared for the sick

called God

Healer.

The slave who was freed from bondage

called God

Redeemer.

The grandfather whose hair was white with the years

called God

Ancient One.

The grandmother who was bent with age and sorrow

called God

Comforter.

The young woman who nursed her newborn son

called God

Mother.

The young man who held the hand of his baby daughter

called God

Father.

And the child
who was lonely
called God
Friend.

All the people called God
by different names.
They tried to tell one another
that their name
was the best,
the only name for God,
and that all other names
were wrong.

But no one listened.
Least of all, God.

And so each person
kept searching
for God's name.

Then one day the person
who called God
Ancient One
and the one who called God
Friend,
the one who called God
Mother
and the one who called God
Father —
all the people
who called God
by a different name
came together.

They knelt by a lake
that was clear and quiet
like a mirror,
God's mirror.

Then each person
who had a name for God
looked at the others
who had a different name.
They looked into
God's mirror
and saw their own faces
and the faces
of all the others.

And they called out
their names for God —
Source of Life —
Creator of Light —
Shepherd —
Maker of Peace —
My Rock — *Healer* —
Redeemer —
Ancient One —
Comforter —
Mother — *Father* —
Friend —
all at the same time.

At that moment,
the people knew
that all the names for God
were good,
and no name
was better than another.

Then all at once
their voices came together
and they called God
One.

Everyone listened.

Most of all,

God.